New Seasons is a registered trademark of Publications International, Ltd.

© 2006 New Seasons®
All rights reserved.
This publication may not be reproduced in whole or in part by any means
whatsoever without written permission from:

Louis Weber, CEO
Publications International, Ltd.
7373 North Cicero Avenue
Lincolnwood, Illinois 60712

www.pilbooks.com

Permission is never granted for commercial purposes.

Manufactured in China.

8 7 6 5 4 3 2 1

ISBN-13: 978-1-4127-5438-5
ISBN-10: 1-4127-5438-0

The GRADUATE'S Guide

to the REAL WORLD

Written by V. C. Graham

new seasons®

Okay, now what?

Finding a full-time job
IS a full-time job.

Some storage units are heated,

right?

Be nice to this guy.

Some day, you'll need him
to recover your data.

Time to hang up your ramen noodles.

The person who hires you to work
in the mailroom may be giving you
the greatest opportunity of all.

Take the change out of your pockets
before doing the laundry.

A cash machine receipt is not
a substitute for a budget.

```
bit-tēr-sweet
    adj
  1: being bitter and sweet at once,
     esp. pleasant but marked with regret
  2: relating to graduation day
```

Ah, the smell of a
freshly sharpened No. 2 pencil.

Sort of brings back Exam Week,
doesn't it?

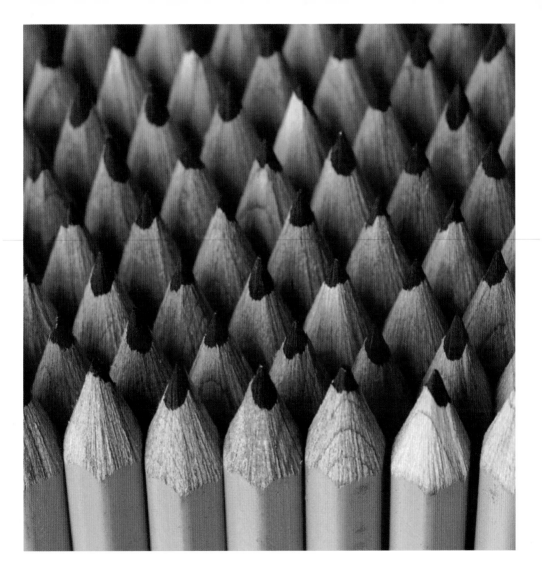

<u>Graduated</u>
does not necessarily mean
<u>domesticated</u>.

Hearing what your classmates
grow up to be is one of life's
longest-running comedies.

You may have survived college boys, but are you prepared to handle 13 crushes in one school year?

You'll know you're a grown-up when you hear yourself say,

"Now who would want to sit in the middle of all that to watch a ballgame when you can watch it on TV in the comfort of your own home?"

Think on the bright side:
It isn't a small apartment —
it is a huge walk-in closet.

It's going to be okay.

Really.

Heck yeah, you want to take it home!

My boyfriend just graduated, and
I'm going to go to the library
every Saturday night.

Sure I am.

After a month of breakfast bars
and leftover pizza,

you're going to miss me.

Be extra nice to your folks
between January 1 and April 15.

They can show you how
to fill out line 8.

are, check here

and enter date final wag-

nal employers on page 1 of the instructions and check her

ehold) employed in the pay period that includes March 12th ▶

	2
	3
	4

compensation

wages, tips, and sick pay

tax for preceding quarters of calendar year

| | 5 |
| | 6 |

withheld (line 3 as adjusted by line 4—see instructions)

$ 28,659 23 | × 12.4% (.124) =

$ | × 12.4% (.124) =

$ | × 2.9% (.029) =

...ck here if wages ▶ ☐

...lanation)

d tips

edicare taxes (add lines 6a, 6b, and

ecurity and/or Medicare tax .

urity and Medicare taxes (see instructions

± Other...

___ ± Fractions of Cents $ _____

l security and Medicare taxes (line 8 as adjusted

5 and 10) ·

ome credit (EIC) payments made to employees, if any ·

12 from line 11). **This should equal line 17, column (d) below**

...pplied from a prior quarter

Service ·

A double mocha latte can bring a
grown man to his knees.

Or his pants to his knees,
at least.

Get your entire body checked now.

In one month the insurance company is
going to drop you like a bad habit.

Remember when you
considered this stressful?

Be sure your mom sees
your fridge like this.

She'll make your dad send money.

'Nuff said.

The one person for whom you
do not open the door will turn
out to be your new boss.

Spring Break.

Sigh.

Remember when you could
just not show up, and
make an excuse later?

That's over.

If you thought sharing a dorm room was tough, wait until you have to listen to this guy call his girlfriend

"snoogy-woogums"

about a million times a day.

When the ride gets bumpy,

just hang on!

If you appear to be enjoying
yourself, sooner or later
you probably will.

Never burn one of these.

Earn your stripes.

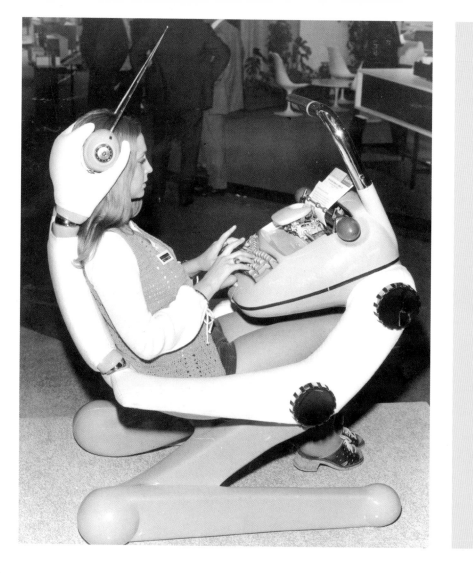

Keep up with technology.

Never be too
old to play.

Now that you are finished with school,
are you ready to begin your

real education?